SECRETS TOP SALESMEN DON'T WANT YOU TO KNOW

Secrets Top Salesmen Don't Want You To Know

Jeffrey Adams Norris

iUniverse, Inc.

New York Lincoln Shanghai

Secrets Top Salesmen Don't Want You To Know

iUniverse, Inc.

For information address:
iUniverse, Inc.
2021 Pine Lake Road, Suite 100
Lincoln, NE 68512
www.iuniverse.com

ISBN: 0-595-28159-1

Printed in the United States of America

Contents

PREFACE

If you are reading this book with the hopes that it will make you a million dollars, please return it to the bookstore where you bought it and get your money back. This book will not help you do so and when you read the chapter on "My Boss is a Sociopath" you will understand why.

What this book will do is help you to increase your commission income to $100,000, $200,000, $300,000, or more a year while maintaining balance in your life. You do not have to become a workaholic and give up all of your free time in order to make this kind of money. You can still have a healthy family life, hobbies, and friends.

I operate a one-man insurance agency out of the basement of my home. My commission income for the last three years placed me in the top 5% bracket of annual income earners. I do this with the help of one woman who does my accounting who only works in the office four days a week. On Mondays she does meals on wheels charity work delivering meals to the sick and homebound in downtown Atlanta. This is part of our corporate desire to return some of our good fortune back to those not as fortunate.

I do not advertise and rarely visit my clients. As a matter of fact, I have not even met about 30% of my clients. A lot of this has to do with the specific type of business I am in but the real question is how can I be this successful with such apparent ease?

The answer is so simple and so obvious that it is hard for me to believe it is not obvious to others. You do not have to buy a battery of cassette tapes or CD's to learn how to become a high producing salesperson. The answer, to me, is just plain common sense. I am still amazed that the common sense secrets that I use are not apparent to everyone.

I really shouldn't be telling you my secrets. By telling you, I just made my job harder because my competition will now be able to do what I do. My competition does such a bad job that is makes my job unbelievably simple. So why even divulge my secrets of success?

The obvious reason is hopefully I will sell a lot of books and be able to get out of the business I am in and dedicate full time to my hobbies and interests. As an insurance agent, the insurance companies that I have to deal with on a daily basis make my life miserable. They do such a horrible job that I hope they too will read this book and clean up their act. I am so tired of dealing with inept and incompetent underwriters that I am about ready to pull out my hair. Please refer to the cover jacket and you will see what they have already done to me.

Hopefully the Insurance companies that I deal with will start to apply the principles set forth in this book and make their life and their customers' life, the insurance agent, more productive. In the meantime, I have had enough and am ready to jump out with my golden parachute.

In my opinion, the state of business principals and ethics in America is appalling. No wonder our economy is in shambles. I am only hard on insurance companies and insurance agencies because that happens to be the particular industry that I am in. One just has to look at the stock market and the state of their 401K's to see how Corporate America lies to its shareholders. In my opinion, the CEO's and their investment bankers just plain lied to everyone. What is going on?

The common sense secrets you are about to learn apply to any industry. I do not care if you are a used car salesman or a medical sales representative for the largest medical supply company in the world. The common sense secrets in this book apply.

As a matter of fact, what you are about to learn will improve your daily life including your personal relationships with your family and friends. Be someone who can look in the mirror and feel good about what they see. Are your ready? Let's rock and roll.

RETURN PHONE CALLS

I am going to start off my book on salesmanship with its biggest gun. A gun so big and so powerful that if you don't read anything else in this book you will already have a huge advantage over your competition. It is my biggest gun in my arsenal and is capable of completely annihilating my competition. I will say it three times in case you miss the first two explosions that should be going off in your head.

BOOM—RETURN PHONE CALLS IMMEDIATELY
BOOM—RETURN PHONE CALLS IMMEDIATELY
BOOM—RETURN PHONE CALLS IMMEDIATELY

I don't care if you follow any other advice in this book. If you RETURN PHONE CALLS IMMEDIATELY you will out perform your competition. Did you hear the cannon thunder or do I need to say it again? BOOM—BOOM—BOOM it is a booming salvo so loud that it should be deafening.

Before I do anything else, if someone calls and I am unable to take the call, I RETURN THEIR PHONE CALL IMMEDIATELY. (BOOM) The only reasons I will not talk to a client immediately are death in the family or I am currently talking to another client. So if I get a phone call and am talking on the other line, Tracy leaves me a message telling me who called. As soon as I am off the phone with the client I am talking to at the moment, I IMMEDIATELY RETURN THE PHONE CALL. BOOM. (Please tell me you heard the cannon blast this time).

Let me define the word "immediately". Immediately does not mean later this afternoon or an hour or two from now. Immediately means within 30 seconds of getting off the line with my other customer. To me this is just common sense courtesy to my client but people do not do it. Remember, 30 seconds is a whole lot closer to immediately than later on sometime today.

When Tracy and I go to lunch we let the answering machine answer our calls. The first thing I do when I return from lunch an hour later is to sit down, pick up all of my messages, and return all of my messages. My clients never mind leaving me a message because they know they will get a call back right after I return from lunch. I can't tell you how many countless times I am told by the client or prospect after IMMEDIATELY RETURNING THEIR PHONE CALL,—BOOM— "thank you for returning my call". Think about that. He is thanking me for returning a call so I can make money from his business. It is so preposterous that it is hard for me to believe it even happens. What is more incredible, he is not thanking me for returning the call right away; he is thanking me for just plain returning his call at all! What is going so wrong in American business practices that prevent people from extending the common courtesy of returning a phone call? Because other salespeople are doing such a pathetic job, it makes my job ridiculously easy.

I get so much new business by being the first one to call back a prospect that I have to laugh. One of my largest accounts came to my agency because I was the first salesperson to call back. The client told me that he called two other agents before calling me and I was the first one to call him back. He did not know any of us, and was not particularly referred to any of the three insurance agencies. I got the business because I was the first one to return his call!

Think how bad things are in American business that people have to thank me for returning their call. A call I should be thanking them for making. To me it is almost common courtesy to your fellow human being to return their call, but people don't seem to understand that. This secret applies to current customers as well as new prospects. I consider all of my current customers new customers and treat them with the same respect and courtesy that I treat a new prospect.

I love to hear someone say to me, "I am just too busy sometimes to return phone calls right away". When I hear this I just consider it as money in the bank. While you are too busy to return your phone calls right away, I am calling the prospect and getting their business.

Stop reading this book right now and think about what you have just learned. How much better would the state of American Business operate if this one simple courtesy were applied universally? You can throw away this book because you now have a weapon in your salesmanship arsenal so powerful that you are almost guaranteed success. But you know what, I got some other juicy tidbits that I think you will enjoy so maybe better hold on to the book for now and read more.

WAIT ON HOLD

This chapter is a short corollary to the previous chapter about RETURNING PHONE CALLS IMMEDIATELY. (Sorry, I just wanted to say it one more time for good measure). I gave up years ago leaving messages on any of my underwriter's voice mail because I knew I would never get a return call. Or if I did it would be so much later that my client, who may be waiting for an answer, starts to get frustrated with my lack of service. I can only provide as good of service as my insurance companies provide me.

Some may say that I am at the blunt end of such bad service because I am just a small independent insurance agency. I am not a major national insurance agency with large national accounts. The big boys are getting the good service because they are producing so much more business than I do with the insurance companies. I wish that was an excuse but I know it not to be so. At one time I was one of the top three producers for an enormous insurance company in their Atlanta office. I still could not get a phone call returned in any kind of timely fashion. Imagine, if this is how they were treating their best producers, how were they treating everyone else?

So no one in America is returning your telephone calls. What are you to do if you want to get anything accomplished? The most powerful tool you have to combat this problem is the "HOLD REQUEST". I know I will not get a call back from my underwriter if I leave a message on his voice mail. I do not want to rely on luck to get through to my underwriter by calling him back over and over through out the day. How unproductive is that?

I very politely ask the operator or his secretary if I can hold on the line until they are available. I often get the response back that it could be a while before the underwriter is available. My usual response is to remark that I don't mind holding and would like to do so. Nine times out of ten they will put me on hold.

Now I could sit there like an idiot and listen to the elevator music playing on hold or find a way of being productive while on hold. So what I do is place the call on speakerphone and work on some item on my desk while I am on hold. I get an incredible amount of work finished while on hold.

Often times I will even talk on the other line with a client while waiting for the underwriter on the line on hold. If I do talk to another client while on hold, I politely inform my client exactly what I am doing and that I will have to call them back if the underwriter comes on the line while I am talking to him. I usually say something to the effect that I have been trying to get through to the underwriter on an important matter for another client but wanted to talk to you and see if I could be of help to you while I wait. I go on to explain that if the underwriter does break in I will call him back immediately (fist time I didn't capitalize those words) after I get off the line with the underwriter. The client always understands because they have learned by now that I will call them back immediately. They also like the fact that I am willing to work so hard for a client to get something done immediately and they can expect that same kind of service if they need something. Usually I can take care of the client way before the underwriter breaks in on the hold line. Use the hold service. It is very effective and you will find that things get accomplished way faster than you would otherwise expect.

I have been operating my little two-person insurance agency for 12 years. In all that time I can think of only two companies that I could feel comfortable leaving a message on their voice mail knowing that they would call me back in a timely fashion. One is my Lloyds' of London Broker who places all of my Lloyd's of London business. The other is a premium assignment company who finances insurance premiums for my clients. It is a wonderful feeling to know that I will be treated with respect and courtesy and get my calls returned in a timely fashion from these two companies. I am now a very large producer for both of these companies. Both treated me properly since the first day I started doing business with them. Could that be why they now have a very large and satisfied producer? It is so obvious it hurts.

It is also a shame that in the last 12 years only one of the two companies who treated me with common courtesy was not even an American company. I can get better service from my broker and Lloyds' of London, who are 4000 miles away, than I can get from my American companies who have offices in Atlanta less than 40 miles away. It just makes me want to scream.

SELL THEM EXACTLY WHAT THEY WANT

This is going to be your second biggest gun in your arsenal. After you return their phone call immediately you are going to sell the client exactly what they want to buy. I am going to repeat this because it is so simple that it might have slipped by. SELL YOUR CUSTOMER EXACTLY WHAT THEY WANT TO BUY.

I tell you, automobile dealerships seem to be breeding grounds for poor salesman. I walked into a Ford dealer near my house and started to look around the lot. I knew exactly what I wanted. I wanted a red Ford F-150 crew cab truck with leather interior, locking power windows, cruise control, and a compass. I wanted the crew cab because the four doors made it convenient to carry passengers. I wanted the locking power windows because I own a Jack Russell Terrier who learned to stamp around on the door handle in my old car until he found the electric down button to open the window. Jack Russell's also shed a lot so the leather interior made it much easier to clean up his hair. I wanted cruise control because I am lazy and a compass because I have a terrible sense of direction. I went on line to a website that told me exactly what the dealer cost was so I was armed with that information when I went to the car lot.

I see young and eager car salesman, with steam shooting out of his nose, approaching me head on from the other side of the lot. He comes up to me and introduces himself as Sam and asks if he can be of any help. I gave him the whole story in three-part harmony and he went inside to check his inventory list. He came back out and told me that they didn't have exactly what I wanted but they had another truck in a different color with the upgraded interior that he could make a good deal on. I looked him straight in the eye and asked, "I'm sorry, did you not hear what I just told you I wanted to buy"? He said he was sorry but they did not have that exact vehicle in their inventory and then reiterated what a good buy the truck was that he was trying to sell me. I then interrupted him before he finished and asked him again, "Sam, did you not hear what it is I want to buy"? He just looked at me with a blank stare.

"Sam", I said, "if you don't have what I want to buy here on your lot can you find me someone who does"? He sort of looked at me slightly dejected and went inside to check the computer. Guess what? Another dealer in Atlanta had exactly what I was looking for and could have it delivered to their lot the next day. Sam looked at me with those hopeful eyes and said to me what I have heard car salesman say to me a million times before, "Jeff, what will it take to get you into this car today"? Translation: how can I get you to buy this car so I can make some money off the sale? I looked him straight in the eyes and told him that I would buy the car right now for $25,000. Of course I knew from going on line that the dealer cost was $27,000 but hey, he asked.

He looked at his little invoice sheet and replied that he couldn't sell it to me for that. I then asked him why he asked me that question if he wasn't able to sell it to me for that. I can't remember what he said but I believe it wasn't very important. I did eventually come to terms with him on the car but I have a feeling he was happy to see me go.

This was a long story to make a point but I think it serves well to illustrate the problem. The easiest thing to sell to someone is to SELL THEM EXACTLY WHAT THEY WANT. I always tell people not to sell what you want someone to have but to SELL EXACTLY WHAT THEY WANT to buy. It is so simple that it is again hard for me to believe that people don't do this. Listen to exactly what the client is telling you he wants to buy so you can sell him exactly what he wants.

If Sam had truly listened to me when I first gave him the whole story he would have stepped inside his dealership, found the truck I wanted, and sold it to me 10 minutes later. The deal would have been done and he would have a very satisfied client. Guess who I would ask for in a couple of years when I went to replace the vehicle? Instead, I had to prod and beg him to sell me exactly what I wanted and I certainly will not come back to him in the future when I am looking to buy another automobile.

Even if Sam gave up his commission to the dealership that had the automobile and make nothing on this sale, guess who I would return to in the future when looking to buy another automobile? I would return to the guy who sold me EXACTLY WHAT I WANTED. But this goes into the content of the chapter on looking at things on a long-term basis so I will save that for a later.

YOU GOTTA KNOW AND YOU GOTTA BELIEVE!

Obviously, it is important to know and believe in your product. I don't mean to pick on poor Sam the Ford Salesman but he didn't know what he had to sell. I asked him many questions about the F-150 Truck that he could not answer. He did not know what different engine sizes it came in or the load carrying capacity of the bed, or how heavy of a boat I could pull with the truck with the smallest available engine. Sam reminded me of what Shultz use to always say in the old Television Comedy Series, <u>Hogan Heroes</u> "I Know Nothing". That is exactly what I don't want to hear. Unless you are gorgeous swimsuit model who can rely on their outstanding good looks to attract my attention, you better know your product and what you have got to sell. Even the swimsuit model will eventually get frustrating to me if she does not know what she is talking about.

Knowing your product includes knowing how your product compares to other like it out there in the market for sale. I want to know if my Ford Truck gets better gas mileage than the comparable Chevrolet Truck. Tell me every reason why I should buy your truck and not someone else's truck. And if there is something bad about my truck, I want to know about that as well. I want to feel like I made an informed decision when I buy your product. If someone has a product that will serve me better than yours tell me so. I will remember what you did for me and come back to you again the next time first before going any-where else.

As a salesperson, I would always rather sell my product to a well-informed buyer than a buyer who is ill informed. Give me a smart customer any day over a dumb one. The dumb one may buy from you this time but they are the one who will be easily swayed by the next salesman who comes along with a story. If your customer is not well informed, then make him so. Take the time to make him understand what he is buying. I do this all the time in my insurance agency. A lot of clients will buy insurance not knowing what it really will and will not cover. It avoids a lot of problems in the future if they fully understand what they are buying. It will also make them feel better about themselves and about you for taking the time to explain any misunderstanding they may have.

I am telling you also right now that, as the Southern Baptist Preacher would say at the Sunday Tent Revival, YOU GOTTA BELIEVE! You have to believe in the product you are selling. You have to truly believe that it is the best product and the right product for the person you are trying to sell it to. If you don't feel that way then what the heck are you doing trying to sell it to someone anyway? Your enthusiasm will come off either fake or genuine depending on whether or not you believe in your product. If you believe it is the best product available your enthusiasm for the product will be infectious to your customer. If you believe in it than I guarantee you they will believe in it. Unless you are the best actor in the world, if you don't believe in what you are selling, it will come across to the customer. Whether through your body language or through your lack of enthusiasm, it will soon become apparent to the customer that you are not a true believer.

Your job as a salesperson is to learn the market and find out what is the best product available. Then go sell that product. What do you think you will gain by selling something inferior? Do you think you will gain long-term relationships with your customers with an inferior product? The second you find something better than what you have for sale; go sell it. Think about it. There is nothing easier to sell than the best product available.

ASSHOLE FEES

This is one of my favorite dirty little secrets. It is short and sweet but nonetheless a very important lesson in human behavior.

We all have the customer or client that just drives us crazy. You cannot be in business without running into this customer. Maybe he is rude or just impossible to please. You will work harder for these clients than any other clients you have and they will constantly threaten to go somewhere else with their business. This is the client who you have bent over backwards to please and be nice to who does not seem to have the words "thank you" in their vocabulary. . Does this sound familiar to you?

I have often thought about just flushing these clients down the toilet because he or she cause me terrible indigestion and makes my life generally miserable. If I did flush them, who am I really hurting? I may feel better for riding myself of the aggravation but I am also flushing income down the toilet when I flush an aggravating client down the toilet. In my opinion, the best way to get even with these clients is to take their money.

I cringe when I see the aggravating customer's name appear on the caller ID. There is always a short debate I have to have with myself as to whether or not I should even answer their call. No matter what it is going to be about, I know it is going to be unpleasant.

Before picking up his call I stop for one brief second and repeat the words in my head, "Asshole Fees", and then pick up the phone with a smile. You see Asshole Fees are what I charge to clients like this in order to justify in my mind even dealing with the sons of bitches.

Asshole fees are the little charges you can charge a client like this in order to pay for the extra aggravation they cause you. No matter what you are selling, there will be a way to charge this guy a little bit more than you would charge your other clients.

I probably should be embarrassed to admit it but I do exactly this. I finance a lot of premiums with a premium finance company for my customers. I have a small swing of interest rates I can charge customers on their finance agreement. Guess which end of the scale the aggravating customer gets and guess which end of the interest scale my favorite clients get?

I still provide the best service to the Asshole clients that is available. I will do a better job for them than any other insurance agent in the industry. They will, however, get charged a higher commission rate and I will make more money from the aggravating client than I will any other client in my book of business.

It seems to me to be a fair exchange. If these clients are going to cause me more aggravation and more work, than I am going to surcharge them for that extra aggravation and work. The extra amount charged may not amount to much more than your other clients. It is the whole psychological exercise that makes this client bearable. The net effect is more money in your pocket. So when one of our Asshole Clients telephones, smile, repeat under your breath the words, "Asshole Fees", and answer the phone.

YOUR BOSS IS A SOCIOPATH

I always try to help explain human behavior by looking at it on a sort of anthropological basis. A lot of our behavior comes from millions of years of natural selection in the human race. To put it simply, the strong survive. Certain traits in certain human beings made their chances of survival greater than others around them. Traits that make one's chance of survival better are then continued in the population through their offspring. It is the simple rules of natural selection as set forth by Charles Darwin.

I am not a psychologist and I am not a scientist. I do feel I am a skilled observer of human behavior and I think a lot of what I am about to tell you is true. Let me give you an example that I always like to use.

It is fairly common knowledge and even joked about that men want to fall asleep after having sex. It happens to me and hopefully I am not the only one. I don't think I am. I have often wondered why this happens. (Not too often now, give me a break) The science magazines that I like to read tell me that man's body produces the exact enzyme after having sex that the brain uses to fall asleep. So there seems to be an actual biological reason for the physiological response. (Thank God for that). But why does this happen to me? What could possibly be the reason?

I have a theory. For millions of years man lived in small groups with usually one dominate male. I call him the alpha male. This is numero uno man at the top of the evolutionary scale. Through the evolutionary process he was gifted with certain traits that made him superior to his fellow competition. As a result, he had first right of selection to all of the females.

The alpha male would do everything in his power to keep the other males in the group from mating with his harem of females. Does this behavior, however, help to guarantee the continuation of the species? What if the alpha male, through a genetic fluke of evolution is stronger than the other males but who happens to also be infertile? This would not be good for the guaranteed continuation of the species.

Through the long process of evolution, the biological trait arose that makes a male fall asleep after mating with the females. While asleep, the subordinate males have their chance to breed with the females. The more mates the females are able to except, the better chance they will have of fertilization. This seems a good explanation (or as my girlfriend would say, excuse) for this biological reaction to a social interaction in the species. This evolutionary imperative may also explain why a female does not fall asleep after mating. The more males she can accept the better chance she will have of impregnation.

Let's apply this theory now to your boss. What biological imperatives from millions of years of natural selection are involved with his behavior? He is the alpha male that has the evolutionary skills to become the leader of the pack. Most of what made the alpha male the head of the pack was his superior strength combined with violent behavior that ruled over the subordinate males. In America it is unacceptable to control your employees by brute force. Since your boss cannot physically pound you into submission, he or she does it through other controlling and possibly threatening behavior.

A lot of the behavior is actually what I believe to be sociopath behavior. The dictionary defines a sociopath as "A person manifesting antisocial behavior patterns or character traits". Believe me, this defines the behavior of my previous boss. These individuals will lie to you, they will cheat you, and they will try to manipulate you into performing whatever job they want you to accomplish. Some bosses will actually try to bully you into submission. They cannot help it. It is their biological imperative to do so. It is not so much the money, it is the biological imperative to be in control of subordinates.

Some bosses actually can control this behavior and channel it to very productive lives and perform great tasks for society. In my opinion, however, this is usually not the case. Look at all of the despots in world history. As the old saying goes, absolute power corrupts absolutely.

Maybe society needs these types of individuals in order to progress. That can all be left for another time and another debate. Just look to see if your boss fits into this mold. He probably does. He wouldn't be the boss if he didn't.

Is he a good guy or is he a bad guy? If he is the bad guy, expect him to take advantage of your abilities every chance he gets. My recommendation is to start looking for another job immediately. He will drain you and steal from you all of the extra income you will make as a result of reading this book. His philosophy will be in direct conflict with the philosophy of this book and you will be at constant odds with him. Think about it. If he is willing to steal from you to justify his ends than he will expect the same behavior of you. Is this how you want to live your life?

If he is one of the few outstanding good guys, consider yourself very fortunate and do whatever it takes to make that company work. They just don't come along that very often so when one does, seize the opportunity.

DON'T BE HIS BEST BUDDY

There is nothing I hate worse than a backslapping, how ya doing, you're my best buddy mobile home salesman pitch. I just met you so don't try to pretend that you are my best friend. This is something the telemarketers always try to pull. I love a telemarketer's opening line, "Hello Mr. Norris, how are you doing today"? That is the exact wrong thing to ask me. I spend the next 15 minutes telling them how my day has been going and what cute little things my dog did over the weekend. They don't really care how I am doing, they just want to sell me something. I, of course, never buy anything from them but if they are going to pretend to care how I am doing then I am going to pretend to tell them. Don't pretend to be my friend if you really are not my friend.

The key word in the last sentence is "pretend". If you are pretending to be my friend your voice or your body language will give you away. Has the light bulb gone on yet? Don't be a fake. It will show.

The secret to selling someone something is to truly make them their friend. Find a reason to sincerely like the person you are about to speak to. If you never sell him a thing, you will leave that office a richer man. You will feel good about yourself because you have made a new friend. You may never call him again but you will have a pleasant memory of your meeting and your conversation. Seems to me that you are richer already.

The big secret that I am trying to pass on to you is how he will react if he feels that you genuinely like him. Your body language and voice will tell him that you like him and you and he will not even realize it. Your affection for him will come across in your whole demeanor toward the prospective customer. He may not buy anything from you. There is a good chance he will recommend you to a friend. Since you are now friends he won't mind giving you the name of some of his friends that might need your service or product.

This is your best basis for referral business. Let's say you were just in Bob's office trying to sell him some new office furniture. You have a good rapport with Bob and things are moving along nicely. After a little discussion it is apparent that Bob can really not afford new office furniture at this time. Bob wants to upgrade his furniture but cannot afford to at this time. Please do not sell Bob something he cannot afford. What kind of friend would do that? But before you leave, ask Bob if he has any friends who might want to upgrade their office furniture. Bob will probably give you one or two names to call. Then go back to your office and call Bob's friends. Let them know that Bob recommended you to them. The snowball effect is incredible.

When I go on a sales call, I look around the client's waiting room or office. Nine times out of ten there will be something on the wall or on the shelf that the customer is proud of. He may have a picture of his daughter in a ballerina outfit or a 1200-pound marlin on his wall. Look around the office; it will be there.

I have a million things I am interested in and can always find something to talk about with a prospect. I went deep sea fishing one time in my life. I caught a 25-pound Cobia off the panhandle of Florida. It was a very exciting time and I had a lot of fun but never went deep sea fishing again. After I shake the prospects hand while looking him in the eye, before I mention anything about what I have to sell, I mention that Cobia fishing trip and what a great time I had. I am not being insincere or trying to buffalo him, I truly had a great time. The natural enthusiasm I portray for that trip will be infectious and he will no doubt share with me one of his exhilarating fishing trip stories. If it is the guy with a picture of his adorable little girl in a ballerina's tutu on the shelf, I will mention one of my favorite movies, White Nights, which was all about the ballet. I might mention the performance of the Nutcracker Suite that I saw downtown 10 years ago and thoroughly enjoyed. Before you know it, you will be friends and begrudgingly dragging yourselves back to the purpose of your meeting.

He is now your friend so treat him like one. You have got something that you think will help to make his life better. It is a great thing to help a friend, even if you make money doing so. It is OK to make money from doing business with friends. All you are really doing is sharing in the wealth you are helping to create for him. Hey, I am not a saint. If I can make someone else's life better and make mine better for doing so, then so be it. He knows why you are there. Don't try to convince him that you are doing this for just his own good. It is not true and it is not sincere and it is not how a friend treats another friend.

I consider all of my customers friends. If I know of a better deal for them I tell them. If they can get the same thing for cheaper, I let them know. I do ask them to come back to me first the next time to give me a chance at their business. They always do. I get a lot of business this way.

BELIEVE IN THE LONG TERM

The state of American Business Ethics is pathetic. Let's face it; we are not in this recession because we are doing such a great job. Enron will now be a separate sub category in the dictionary under the word greed. Communism was a terrible failure, but I am not convinced that free enterprise has been such a resounding success either. There is enormous room for improvement.

One of the biggest problems, in my opinion, in today's market is the question, "How did the stock do today"? The questions we should be asking is, "How will the stock be doing ten years from now"? Every decision being made in corporate America today is made in hopes of increasing the stock value tomorrow. No one is looking to the future and it is now obvious by the mess the economy is now in.

As a salesperson, you have to find someway to look beyond today and try to see into the future. Maybe the fast hustle will get you the sale today, but where will that client be in the future? Is he going to come back to you? Maybe I have to make certain concessions in my commission on a new account and make half of what I ordinarily would make on a similar sale. I would rather have half of the commission for the next ten years than 100% of the commission for one year.

I don't know how to make a million dollars over night. Very few of us do and I believe it to be a waste of time to direct your efforts toward this end. What I do know is how to build a sales platform so that in ten years you are respected in your field and making a very good living.

I do no advertising. All of my business comes as a result of direct referrals from other clients. It took me 10 years to build my book of business to where it is today. I have gone after certain accounts for 7 years before finally getting them. I have helped some friends with insurance problems without ever writing their business. My first client of ten years ago is still with me. These are all long-term actions and results.

I want to be the kind of person who can get up every morning and look in the mirror and like what I see. Be in the game for the long run. There are no get rich gimmicks that really work. I want to have balance in my life and to enjoy life. It is really more fun to do so.

I don't want to be rich. Believe me, I have known some very wealthy people. They own huge houses, yachts, ranches, and airplanes. I watched one very wealthy friend of mine manage his life. You know what he was doing most of the time? He was trying to take care of all of his stuff. His yacht captain quit so he was looking for a new captain. He needed a new place that he felt more comfortable handling his aircraft maintenance. The contractor building his 12,000 sq. ft house was driving him crazy. He had so much stuff that he was spending all of his time taking care of it.

I want you to learn to look at the long term in everything that you do. This is just not for increasing you sales book. This is an approach that will help you to improve your whole life. Make one of your long-term goals in life to have balance. You might not ever own a 60-foot yacht but you might have a lot more friends come over to your house for a barbecue.

I once read that a survey question asked of 1000 elderly people. The survey covered the entire socioeconomic spectrum. The question put to them was, "What is the most important thing in your life"? The answer was with almost no exception, "friends". The truly rich man is not the man who dies with the most toys. It is the man who dies with the most friends.

ELIMINATE LAYERS OF FAT

Almost every day I hear news reports about Americans getting fatter and fatter. Something like 70% of America is overweight! It never ceases to amaze me how much money the diet industry is making. Let me understand correctly, if I buy your product, I will loose weight? Well I have got some swampland I would like to sell you after you enroll in your latest weight loss program.

Please admit it. Most people are fat because they are lazy. If you want to lose weight, please eat less, eat real food like fruits and vegetables, and exercise more. There, I just saved you $79.99 by your not having to sign up for that new and amazing weight loss program.

Corporate America is also getting lazy and has way too many layers of fat. It is very frustrating for me to call one of my insurance companies and hunt down my underwriter. First I get the switchboard, then I get my underwriter's assistant, and then finally I get put into his voice mail. Since he will never call me back, I have to go through the whole routine again and ask to be put on hold when I get back to the underwriter's assistant again. America, you are making it too hard to do business with you.

There are two layers of fat that can be eliminated in the previous example. I want a direct line to the person I want to speak to. If he is not available, let it roll over into his voice mail. I am only comfortable saying this if I know for a certainty that he will call me back right away after leaving a voice mail. Think how much money companies could save by eliminating these layers of fat. All we have to learn is how to return phone calls.

I am still a little confused about why insurance companies and insurance agencies need so many assistants. I did both jobs and I know how much of a workload they are handling. Most insurance agencies would have two assistants helping me handle the book of business I manage all by myself. You sold the business based on the fact that you would handle the business. Don't be lazy; handle it!

When the phone rings in our office, I answer the phone. Guess what, it is usually someone who wants to talk to me and not to my assistant. (Which I don't have anyway) I know that sounds obvious, but companies would have two people answer the phone before I do.

I can always tell how fat a company is getting by how many meetings they are having. If the management staff of a company always seem to be in meetings, it is a sure sign that the company is about to have a heart attack. When I was an underwriter for an insurance company I sat through more meetings that accomplished absolutely nothing that I was ready to blow my brains out. The translations for, "I'm sorry he is in a meeting", is "sorry, no one is capable of making a decision". The big chiefs all have to meet with the middle chiefs to see how the little chiefs are managing the few remaining working Indians.

In my little two-person operation, Tracy handles all of the accounting and I handle all of the insurance. We have not had a meeting for eight years. I guess I am just too busy doing the work to have meetings.

One little side note that I want to mention here because this seems as good of a place to mention it as any. Never, and I say it again, Never let your phone answer a call with a busy signal. If you can't get the call, make sure it rolls over into a mailbox. If I hear a busy signal when I call a company, I hang up and call another company who will answer their phone. It is my understanding that Federal Express will not let a phone ring more than two times without someone answering it. I have an account with Federal Express and I test them every time I call them for a package pick-up. It never rang more than twice in the seven years I have been checking on them. And every time it is someone who can help me. Hey, what does one of the most successful companies in America know anyway?

YOUR CUSTOMER IS STEAMING MAD

You just picked up the telephone and the receiver is smoking red hot because on the other end of the line is your customer and he is steaming mad. There are many ways to handle this problem. The one way not to handle this problem is to get steaming mad back at your customer. Realize first he has just been promoted to the Ass Hole commission scale and then move on to solve the problem.

My experience tells me that nine times out of ten he is mad about something because he does not understand something. I had a customer call me screaming mad one time because the insurance company had not yet paid off his claim. "They are really dragging their feet on this one. They want their premium right away but when it comes to paying me for my loss they take their sweet f*!ing time." I told the client that I did not understand what was taking so long and that I would call the insurance company immediately and find out what was going on. Turns out that the client had never signed and submitted the final "proof of loss" agreement required in all claims settlements by every insurance company in America. It was sitting on his messy, unorganized desk for two weeks. I called him back immediately and explained in as nice a way as I could that he had failed to do what he had been told two weeks earlier in order to get his money. He mumbled something under his breath that I could not understand and responded that he would sign and fax in the form. This was an easy one because it was his fault.

The really hard ones are the ones in which you made a mistake and you caused the problem. Let's say in the previous example the customer had in fact faxed you the signed proof of loss form two weeks ago. It was your desk that it had been lost on for two weeks and it was your fault that the claim was not paid. What do you do?

This is the perfect opportunity to build the character and reputation you want to have as a businessperson. No matter how hard you try in your endeavors to do a good job, you will make mistakes. Let's face it, we are all human and we are all going to make mistakes. It is a fact of life so get use to it.

What the client does not want to hear is some lame excuse. I know when I am mad I don't want to hear a sorry excuse that does not justify why someone did not do the job they were suppose to do. Grow up and take responsibility for your mistakes.

First thing you do is own up to the mistake. Tell your client you are sorry and you will work on the problem immediately to get it corrected. The second you get off the phone with the customer is when you start working to fix the mess you made. Start the clock. You should be calling back that client with a solution or fix to the problem within an hour. He will start to believe in you again if you do so.

If the opportunity presents itself and if it is a client who actually has a sense of humor, I always use the following line, "Sir, the problem was my fault. I have no real good excuse for my actions. Give me a couple of days and I will come up with a good excuse but for right now, I just plain did not do what I told you I would do." What can they say? You admitted you were wrong, you admitted you made a mistake, you admitted taking responsibility for your actions, and you are going to do everything you can to fix the problem? I usually get a mild laugh as a response.

Turn this whole thing into something positive. First you fix the problem immediately, which shows the client your concern. You didn't patronize the customer with some weak excuse that he doesn't really care about anyway. Because you admitted fault, which very few people do, the client will actually go away from the whole experience with more respect for you than he did when he first called you with the problem. Mistakes can actually work in your favor if you handle them properly. Mistakes can actually strengthen a relationship between your client and you.

SOME LIE BETTER THAN YOU CAN TELL THE TRUTH

This is a relatively new revelation for me. It is one of the saddest diseases that is now an epidemic in American Business. Maybe it has always been there and I was too naive to see it. In either case it is a problem that hurts us all. I see it now all the time with other agents who are trying to compete for my business. Boy did I have a big lesson to learn.

I had an insurance customer who had a small fleet of twin axle pickup trucks used as support in his business. Because of some recent contracts the client was awarded in other states, he had to drive these trucks all over the United States. The current carrier was unable to write this new interstate exposure and asked me to replace the automobile portion of this account. Because the account was so small, I had a terrible time trying to get coverage for this new exposure. My client contacted another agent who was pursuing him for his business to see if he could be of help. Sure enough, that other agent found some coverage when I could not. The unbelievable thing to me was that the other agent wrote the business with a company I had already contacted who declined the business to me. They declined the business to me because of the interstate exposures that I reported to them.

I was totally befuddled. My client was so happy with the other agent that he would barely speak to me. He did however let me look at the submission by the other client to the insurance company who had previously turned me down. I looked at the applications that the agent submitted and like a hot blinding light I saw what the other agent had done. On the application he lied to the insurance company and said that all of the trucks operated within a 50-mile radius of the client's home base. He was off by only about 2500 miles!

This agent not only lied to the insurance company but he lied to the client when he told him he could get him the proper coverage. The client may not have been covered at all. If he had an accident in California while he was suppose to be based in Georgia, the insurance company had every right to decline the claim for a material misrepresentation on the application. This other client had actually put my client and his whole business in jeopardy by lying on the insurance applications. Like I said, he lied better than I told the truth.

You would think that my client would jump up and down screaming mad about how this agent put his whole business in peril by lying to the insurance company. But you know what he did? He moved the rest of the business he had with me to the new agent! My client didn't care that this new agent lied. It still floors me when I think about this.

It was a big fat lesson to me that I had not yet learned. People lie and they lie all the time. The sad part is that most of them get away with it too. You just have to choose how you want to live your life. I lost about $50,000 annual commission on this account because I would not lie to the insurance company. If my client had an accident there was a chance that the company would never refer back to the original applications to notice the disparity in information presented to them. Maybe they would check and I could not take that chance with someone who had put their trust in me. A lot of people seem to get away with a whole lot of lying. I have decided that I do not want to live my life this way. In this one case it cost me $50,000 a year.

I still have a theory that a salesperson will make more money in the long run by always telling the truth. To me it just seems good business to always tell the truth. This is the basis on which I built my book of business. If someone is willing to lie to you it is just a matter of time before it will catches up with him. I truly believe this and hope that I am correct. The jury is still out on this study and I will let you know what answer I find.

SOLVE A PROBLEM

You want to know a great way to write new business. Solve a problem. Do not go after the easy account because I am telling you right now, you are not going to get it. What can you really do better than someone else on something that is easy to accomplish? I often ask a new prospect if he is married to his current salesperson. I want to find out what the relationship is between the two of them. If the potential client loves his current agent and is ecstatic with their service and product, just shake his hand, say thank you for seeing me, and walk out. If there is a happy long-term relationship between the prospect and his current salesperson, you are not going to break them up. Translation: You are wasting your time; you will not get the business.

If I do hear, however, that he is unhappy with his current salesperson, I attack that opening like a starving coyote attacks a baby sheep. Can you hear what he is saying to you? You better listen because if you do not listen someone else will. What he is really saying is, "if you can solve my problems and make my life better, you can have my business". You now have almost a 100% chance of writing his business or selling him your product if you can in fact solve his problem.

The next question out of your mouth better be, "what exactly is your problem"? This man is a friend of yours now and you sincerely want to help him. Get in excruciating details the exact nature of his problem and write notes as he speaks to you. Make sure you get down everything concerning the problem. He may have one big obvious problem. He probably also has two or three little problems related to the one big problem. Make sure you solve all of his problems not just the obvious one.

What you are actually doing is pre-qualifying the prospect. I never bother with a prospect if he has no problems. I only want prospects with problems because I know that nine times out of ten, I will write the business. There is no such thing as a problem. Someone just has not yet found the solution.

I use to work out at the local health club. I became work out buddies with a woman who also frequented the gym on a regular basis. We never saw each other outside of the health club. Because we were in close proximity to one another during work out classes, we would often times strike up a conversation. After a couple of years we actually became health club buddies and talked frequently. She knew I was an insurance agent and I knew she was a rental agent for a large real estate investment trust company that owned about 100 shopping centers. One day she came to me lamenting that their risk manager had just quit and the insurance program had been thrown into her lap. CHA-CHING

She was dealing with their current insurance agent. I could tell that she was not really happy with him. She said that he talked down to her because she knew so little about insurance. She was also unhappy because it took five insurance companies to write her company's insurance program. One company wrote the property insurance, another wrote the liability insurance, another wrote the umbrella, another wrote the workers' compensation, and another wrote her business auto insurance. Now this sounds crazy but that is how the insurance market works. Some companies are more competitive on property coverage and some companies are more competitive on the liability side. Sounds crazy but it is true.

I asked her if I could be of any help? She said that she would really like to try and work with her if I could help her straighten out her problems. First thing I did was to be clear on her problems. She had two problems: She didn't understand insurance and her current coverage was scattered over five different insurance companies.

For the next three months I spent hours and hours with her going over each and every one of her insurance policies at her office. She started to become comfortable with the insurance program, which solved the first problem. The second one proved a little more daunting to solve.

After going to a number of insurance companies I finally came across an underwriter at one of the large national insurance companies who could actually think a little outside of the box. His company was competitive on the liability insurance and the umbrella insurance but not so competitive on the other coverage's. With just a little help on my part, he learned what it would take to be competitive on the entire insurance program. We built a comprehensive insurance program with the one insurance company. The client, who was now comfortable with her knowledge of insurance, loved the program. I wrote that account for many years and it ran like a well-oiled clock. It was a thing of beauty.

The account paid $75,000 a year in commission. Not bad for a guy who been an insurance agent for only two years who barely had a book of business. Build it and they will come.

GO AFTER THE BIG FISH

Let me ask you a very simple question. When you go Marlin deep-sea fishing do you go out hoping to catch a nice little 200-pound Marlin? Or are you like me? I want to put the biggest damn hook of the line to go out and catch me the biggest damn Marlin in the world. I mean I want to catch the 1200 fish that takes me three hours to land and get in the boat. I want to catch a Marlin that will break the world record for largest Marlin ever caught in the world.

Think about it now. What do you do different to catch a 1200-pound Marlin versus a 200-pound Marlin? The answer is, almost absolutely nothing different. You still have to rent the boat, you still have to ride miles off shore, and you still put the same bait on the hook. The only difference is that it might take you a little extra time to reel in the big fish. I'm telling you right now, don't be afraid to go after the big fish.

I have a friend, Joey, who is a perfect example for everyone. Joey sells furniture wholesale. He sells the inexpensive rattan furniture that everyone has on their back porch. Think how hard it must be to make money on furniture that someone can buy a whole set for just a few hundred dollars. Joey sells this stuff by the trainload and he sells it to the biggest retailers in the United States. One of those retailer's name starts with a K but I cannot say whom it is.

I once asked Joey about his secrets to his success. "Joey", I asked, "There are thousands of guys out there all trying to sell the same inexpensive furniture that you sell. Tell me why is it that you are able to sell to the largest retailers in the whole country while the other 999 sales-men can't"?

I asked Joey this question over 20 years ago and I have never forgotten his answer. Joey looked at me with his smiling eyes and answered, "Jeff because I am not afraid to talk to them". That was it; there was no more to his explanation. The answer was so simple and so pure it was beautiful.

I took to heart his answer and found it to be absolutely true. When I developed the shopping center insurance program that I talked about in the last chapter, I was really excited about its potential. I called every real estate investment trust that owned a schedule of shopping centers in the United States. I went down the list starting from the very biggest in the entire United States to the one ranked number 20 in size. Because I had solved a problem that I now realized everyone in the United States had with multiple companies handling their insurance, every single one of them was willing to talk to me. I was flying all over the United States giving presentations in the headquarters of these large companies. I had the right bait and I was going after the biggest fish in the sea. The heck with Marlin fishing, I wanted to catch me a whale!

Everything was going great. I had some enormous insurance programs on my desk that I prepared for my underwriter. He was excited and I was excited. Than, without warning, the worst hurricane to ever hit the State of Florida, Hurricane Andrew, swept across its borders. It leveled half of Southern Florida and the losses almost bankrupted some of the largest insurance companies in the world. Two days later, my program was shut down as a consequence of the devastation Hurricane Andrew had caused to my insurance carrier.

I learned a very important lesson. Do not be afraid to go after the big fish. You do, however, have to keep everything is perspective. I am a two-man operation and I do not have the staffing to handle an account like General Electric but I am capable of handling medium size companies. So I go after the big fish I know I can catch and leave the blue whales for the companies that can handle them.

The corollary to this secret is, "You get the business you go after". Sounds simple but a lot of salesmen miss this point. I do not do any personal lines insurance business like homeowners and private automobile insurance. I do not do it for a favor for my good clients. I do not have a contract with an insurance company who will allow me to write personal lines business. I only do small to medium size commercial business insurance. And guess what kind of business I have written the last 10 years: small to medium size commercial business.

I see many a salesperson fall into this trap. They will do a favor for someone at one of their customers or for one of the employees. Maybe they agree to place a personal automobile policy for the vice-president of the company. Next thing they know other employees swamp them with requests to provide the same favor. Can you guess what happens next? They are drowning with favors that take up enormous amounts of time with very little return. Pick the business you want and go after that business and stick to that business.

If you go after the easy stuff that provides little return that is exactly the kind of business you will have in your book of business. Remember, it takes just a little longer to land that 1200-pound marlin and you can eat for a lot long time off that big fish.

TECHNOLOGY SAVES

Technology is my new religion. I stand at the Alter of Technology every morning and ask to be blessed with its miracles. There are wondrous things out there that can make your job more productive. Seek them out and become a disciple of their teachings. I think I will put a fish symbol on the back of my car with the word "Technology" in the middle of the pendant.

One of my biggest pet peeves is the amount of time wasted sending and receiving faxes. The amount of time and productivity wasted getting up from your desk, going to the fax machine, and then doing the whole thing in reverse when a fax is received is incredible. I don't care if you are actually doing it or your secretary is doing it for you, someone is wasting time.

Here is how I have my desk set up. I, of course, have the ever-present desktop computer working at my desk station. My new computer has a flat screen monitor, which saves me an incredible amount of space on my desk. The only other pieces of hardware I have on my desk are a two-line phone and a scanner. I don't use a flatbed scanner because they take up way to much space. I have what is called a desktop scanner that is about 10 inches long and three inches deep. Anything I scan goes through the roller in the scanner and comes right back at me. The phone has all of my clients numbers in its memory so I never waste time looking up phone numbers or dialing phone numbers.

The scanner and the desktop computer double as my fax station. I have a separate phone line coming into my office that is a dedicated fax line.

My scanner, and Tracy's scanner are hooked up to that dedicated line. I never get up from my desk to either send or receive a fax. Any received fax comes through my fax program and is printed out on the printer right next to my desk. If I want to send a fax, I scan it in through the desktop scanner and send it right from my desk. The fax program has all of my clients fax numbers in it so all I do is scan in the paper, hit a button, and it is gone. Then I just instruct the fax program to print out any additional information I sent on the cover page and put it in the file.

If I am working in my word processor writing a letter, I never mail it to the client, I fax it. I fax it right from the word processor program directly to the client. Because it is never scanned the client's fax machine becomes a printer and the letter prints out on his fax machine looking like an original. How much time and money have I just saved by not mailing a letter to the customer? Nobody cares anymore that they are not getting originals in the mail so why are you sending things that way?

Tracy, who does all of the accounting work for our agency, has not mailed out an invoice in years. When we know what to bill a customer, she faxes the original invoice to the customer immediately. I have not been asked for an original invoice for the last five years. There are even programs that will fax the invoice and do all of the accounting work that the invoice generates immediately as part of the program. You can now do in less time what it took more people longer to accomplish before if you just apply the available technology.

I am obviously a believer in technology. All of my clients are in my certificate program. If a client calls me requesting a certificate evidencing coverage, I open up my certificate program and punch out the certificate as soon as I get off the phone. I fax an original certificate to their office, print out one for my hard file, and am finished in five minutes. Think about it, from the time they made their request to the time the certificate is arriving in their office is five minutes! Are you providing this kind of service? Thanks for making my job easy.

Do not fight technology; embrace it. It gives you the edge that makes the difference between keeping and losing a customer.

MAKE SERVICE A GAME

This is a brief corollary to the previous chapter "Technology Saves". Technology saves only if you use it once you got it. All the computing power in the world doesn't help one bit if it is sitting on your desk at idle all of the time. Use it to provide a level of service excellence that even amazes your customers.

I play a little game in my head the minute I pick up the phone to talk to a client. I hear what he wants and ask myself how can I get it accomplished as quickly as possible. I like to engage the customer in a bit of a conversation after he tells me what he wants. While we are catching up on the local gossip, I am calling up what he needs in the computer. A lot of times the customer is just looking for a copy of a certificate or a form of some kind or another. So while we are chatting I am faxing him exactly what he is requesting. Then just before we are about to hang up I love to tell the customer that he needs to go and check his fax machine because what he had just requested is sitting there waiting for him. They love it.

If it is a request I cannot get accomplished while we are talking on the phone I try to get what he needs as fast as I can. I hang up, grab his file, and using the techniques I already spoke of, try to get what he needs in the next five minutes.

I even have my files organized and my office organized to better suit this purpose. The filing cabinets with all of my accounts are right next to my desk. My files are all organized like they were blue prints for the moon-landing mission. If a client lost something I sent to him 8 months ago, I can go right to that date in my files and fax it to him from my desk. If my client lost a fax I sent to him 6 months ago, I go to that date in my computer fax file and hit resend. I have about 100 little gimmicks I set up in my office to try and decrease the time it takes me to provide the customer with exactly what he is requesting.

You can only accomplish a task as fast as those you have to work around. That is why I had to write this book. The reason I can usually not provide the kind of service that I want to provide is because someone else is not doing the same kind of job I am doing. If I can get everyone working the way I do, it just makes my job easier and ultimately the customer's job easier. I believe running your business like I am suggesting would drag the United States out of its current recession. Productivity would increase so dramatically that we would spring board ourselves back into prosperity.

24 / 7 / 52 / 10

I have either worked or been on call every day for the last 10 years. I am not kidding. There has not been one day that I was not available to my customers. Even when I was attending my best friend's wedding in Nassau in the Bahamas, I talked to a client every day. Now I didn't spend the whole day on the phone while I should have been basking in the sun. I am not that much of a workaholic. I did however check twice a day with the office to make sure I did not need to call someone. Sorry but this is the kind of devotion it will take to become one of the best salesmen in your company. Prepare to work or be on call 24 hours a day, seven days a week, 52 weeks a year, for 10 years.

It really is not as bad as it sounds. I forward my office number to my cellular phone and wear that where ever I go when I am not in the office. Since I consider most of my customers my friends, I really don't mind talking to them after work or on the weekends. I can't tell you the number of times I had to quit what I was doing and drive back to the house to help my customer with whatever it was they needed.

I like to water ski and sometimes I am out on the boat in some secluded cove miles from my house making a few runs when the phone rings. If I am behind the boat, I complete the run and immediately pick up any message left on my voice mail.

If the customer leaves a message that he needs to talk to me, I call him right there from the boat. The customer will be amazed that you even bothered to call him back because nobody else does. He will more than likely apologize for interrupting your weekend. He's your friend and he knows what he is asking of you. Nine times out of ten it is not a real emergency that has to be handled immediately. I had an old boss that use to tell me, unless someone is lying in the road bleeding, there is no such thing as an emergency.

When you call back the client, determine what kind of rush he really is in. Tell him the truth. Bob, I am out in the middle of the lake making a few ski runs but will drive the boat back right now to send you that information. More times than not he will reply that it isn't a real emergency but if he could get it within the next couple of hours that would be great. Everyone is happy. You get to work for a few hours on your tan and he gets what he needs a few hours later. His needs are met as well as yours and the customer will love you for it.

I tell everybody that I really don't work hard. I just work all of the time. There is a big difference. It pays off.

EPILOGUE

As we say in the South, you are now loaded for Bear, so go kill you a bear! Trust me, these few habits that are discussed in this book will make a world of difference to you and to your pocketbook. Try it and see.

I hope, however, that this book does more than just line your pockets with gold. I hope it will make you want to be a better person as well as a better salesman. It amazes me to think how being a better person enriches your life in so many ways. The pot of gold is out there for you and if you get it by using the techniques in this book, than I feel that you deserve it.

Have a lot of fun and look forward to my next book:

More Secrets Top Salesman Don't Want You To Know.

Jeff Norris

0-595-28159-1

www.ingramcontent.com/pod-product-compliance
Lightning Source LLC
Chambersburg PA
CBHW021040180526
45163CB00005B/2209